O MAK
OF CANOES

AN ANTHOLOGY OF POEMS
FROM THE WHITE EAGLE LODGE

WHITE EAGLE PUBLISHING TRUST
NEW LANDS : LISS : HAMPSHIRE : ENGLAND

INTRODUCTION

This booklet grew out of the idea of bringing together some of the poems that have appeared over the years in the White Eagle Lodge magazine STELLA POLARIS. *We planned also to include a selection of the many evocative woodcuts and scraperboard drawings that were such a feature of the older issues of* STELLA POLARIS, *and of its predecessor* ANGELUS. *As the small collection began to take shape, we found several other poems, written by those involved in White Eagle's work, but never actually appearing in* STELLA POLARIS, *that we now had a special opportunity to print.*

The poems of course cover many different subjects, but what we feel they have in common is that each in some way offers a personal reflection of trying to tread the path of spiritual awareness that White Eagle has opened for us. There is a section of poems (pp 18-21) that actually talk about meditation, but others are very much about the writer's outer experience - and yet as the writer describes a scene, or talks about an experience, what he or she has eventually evoked is finding there, in a personal way, an inward path of beauty and love, 'that unsuspected path in your very midst'. We feel that all the poems, different as they are, record something the writer has perceived - or come to feel as they wrote - with sincerity and fidelity: qualities not always easy to achieve. In this way may they be enjoyed, and may they be together a witness to something of the beauty of the greater life which it has been White Eagle's work to reveal.

In bringing together this booklet, we have aimed for variety, but also to include enough poems by the main authors represented to give it coherence - the booklet is not at all meant to be a 'twenty best poems'.

It has been an enjoyable and relaxing task to sift through the illustrations that have been contributed to STELLA POLARIS *over the years. Although we have tried to choose drawings that are in harmony with the particular poems, they are not intended actually to illustrate them. Like the poems they are there just to be looked at - or read - in their own right.*

We are grateful for the permission given by the authors of the poems for their work to be included - and also to all those who have written for STELLA POLARIS *over the years.*

May this little book bring pleasure to many.

JEREMY HAYWARD

INVOCATION

O Maker of Canoes, how shall I build Thy Boat?

*   *   *

Take from the tree, its living bark pulsating,
    Strength:
And from the steel-cold stream by which it watches,
And from the blue, flood meadow waters, falling,
    Peace.
Take from the cloud-barred, golden moon, ascending,
    Light:
And from the stars in silver-pointed pattern,
And from the rain-washed, winter twilight, cooling,
    Calm.

*   *   *

O Tree, thy strength I wield,
O Stream, thy waters heal:
The peaceful meadow stands;
Yet nothing have I taken.
I touch not with these hands
The water's cold-blue steel.
The tree waits in the field
Its boughs by me unshaken.
The gold climbs in moonbeams,
The silver starpoint gleams,
The twilight keeps its hour.
From these I draw the power.
O Maker of Canoes, all these I take are Thine,
Yet nothing have I now that was not ever mine.

                                            TEDDY DENT

HYMN

Have you seen the apple blossom
Falling like the grace of God?
Have you walked the orchard garden
Where my questing feet have trod?

Where I stand, the clouds of glory
Cluster white above my head
As I wait to take the blessing
Of their petals, slowly shed.

Cool beneath, the grass is dewy;
Every blade has life and sings
As this perfect benediction
Falls and falls on pure, white wings.

Here I stand, O Lord of Beauty,
In this garden where Thou art;
May the glory of Thy presence
Blossom, too, within my heart.

TEDDY DENT

WATERLOO STATION, THE BAR - MAY 1943

Those who have read Grace Cooke's book MEDITATION will be familiar with Teddy Dent as the author of the poems 'The Lake of Peace' and 'O God, where beauty is, Thou art'. Most of his poems were in fact written during the Second World War, often while he was on fire-watch duty in London, and this poem records a picture of wartime London.

The child crying,
The strained face pressing,
The quick light of the heart breaking through:
All these are part of me and I in them,
Holding the current of life.
In the heart there is unity
And all before me are God and myself.

The stumbling sailor,
The barmaid with her patient smile,
The youngster drunk with youth and heady comradeship
From glass to glass.
The time-wise sergeant watching him, as I watch,
Steadfast in sympathy and understanding.

The laughing pilot,
Drowning his dreams of strain that's pitiless
Until the tired release of action breaks
The spirit's steeled intensity.
The wife's love-hallowed mask, unhappy-smiling
To ward the bitterness to come
And all too soon to break again -
And then eternally again until there's peace at heart
Or numbed life that's unlived.

The tired old woman, without uniform,
But not without the war's scarred heart within,
Spending alone in crowded solitude

A little for oblivion's gentleness,
Before the long-houred day that waits
Past youth's dear loveliness and richly borrowed time.

All these are mine by kinship and by blood
That beats in me and all the life He made
That we might know.

That we might know and might become,
Out of the striving dark of mind and body pitiful,
Out of the narrow prison of the breast,
Out of the ancient lures of earth and self-forgetfulness:
Out of all things unreal,
The perfect image of His being,
Man.

                                        TEDDY DENT

MEDITATION

It was at the wild edge of the garden
That place,
Where meadow grass lengthens towards
The dappling light,
And the trees grow closer.
Not yet a wood,
The light still falling more than shade,
Even in full leaf of summer.

There was no one there,
Though countless elementals
Were at their loving work,
And birds accompanied their hidden song.
There was only the grass and the trees,
The sunlight,
And eternal stillness,
So deep and full
That it was All.

PAT DACRE

THE ANGEL TO THE BABY

Can you hear me, my friend?
Now you are born,
Enshrouded in form,
I will not leave you,
Lying in the cradle of earth,
In the wrinkled, soft, new home of flesh,
I will help you grow,
When you no longer remember your wings,
I will lend you mine.

Can you hear me, my friend?
Here so recently,
Now without memory,
I will not leave you,
Clothed in the mantle of earth,
You will sense me
In the eyes of your mother,
Or a forest's shaded silence,
In a petal's curled perfection,
Or the colour of a sky.

Can you hear me, my friend?
Sleeping again,
Beginning again,
I will not leave you,
Drawn to the schoolroom of earth,
I will guide you
To the stillness in your heart
When the world is cruel,
To your soul's flame
When the beast roars;
In love, I will be your balance,
In pain, the cool water of peace.

Can you hear me, my friend?
Nestled in time,
By Love designed,
I will not leave you,
Held in the pull of earth,
I will sing to you
In the shadows of the trees
On a day when you are tired,
Through the melody of summer
When you are old,
And you will find me waiting
On the edge of your dreams,
And your tears, and your prayers.

Can you hear me, my friend?
Wiser than infancy,
Stronger than death,
I will not leave you.

PAT DACRE

THE GARDENER

'This poem began in praise of a friend of mine who is a landscape gardener. He works and lives in a community in the New Forest which exists to offer time and space in beautiful surroundings to those in need, free of charge. However, as I wrote, the gardener became He who nurtures the gardens of our souls, and the poem became something other than I had intended.'

He watches the daylight circling the house,
Gently pacing the grass and tired borders of our neglectful years.
In the soft shade by the willow nettles abound,
and couch grass deepens its roots in forgotten corners,
Yet, to His eyes, comfrey's flower-bells and the rosy haze of
                                                                     honesty
Infuse this fallow ground with hope.
We follow His path to the starry-blue of speedwell in our
                                                                meadow lawn,
And, where the stream loses its way in mud, He bends to
                                                                reveal the lily.

Yesterday our land fretted under jaundiced eyes,
And sometime in the darkness we faced our need;
The road, disused, lying in the long shadows of the wall.
We awoke to find Him there, where the path divides,
Touching wallflowers and wild violets with His smile.

Now He walks across the terrace where the dandelions reflect
                                                                   the sun,
And finds tight coils of ancient ferns unfolding to the light,
And, as He passes through the archway to the summer house
                                                                   beyond,
We remember the rose, and hurry to its resurrection.

                                                                       PAT DACRE

A WINTER SEA

The waters of the sea call to my soul,
Echo in the tides of my blood.

The blue crystals of foam
Splintering along the shore,
And along the shore, piercing my heart,
This restless beauty breaks,
Filling the air, my breath,
With the ancient stream and pull of waves.

And out over the greening deeps
This crystal surface shivers light into a million flashing gems:
The blazing suns of space, or nuclei of cells,
Floating, resounding, pebble-like skimming
Through the spray-filled, distant range,
Where shadows chase the tails of white combers
Across a chameleon cocoon.

And here, where all should be at rest,
My blood lurches to follow the billows' rioting wake,
Eventually to break, in endless joy,
Surrender, upon God's waiting shore.

PAT DACRE

A WALK IN THE WOODS

O red-brown pines,
Making your own music beneath the wind's voice,
The quiet of your branches
Has crept past the quarrelling sentries of thought
And led the prisoner heart to the well of peace.

JEREMY HAYWARD

THE CHRISTMAS ROSE

In this time of quietness,
Of stillness and deepening snow,
In the secret roots of earth
The rose of light will grow.
All is withdrawn
To that inward holy place,
Where shafts of fire and air
A heavenly pattern trace.

Essence of light below
The dead leaves, stones and bark,
This is the mystery
Held in the winter-dark.
Through frost and shadow and cold
The pilgrim travels far
To find the child asleep
In the heart of the golden star.

JOAN PUNCHARD

RENEWAL

From winter, from shadow and dusk
Is formed this lovely thing,
Flame of crystal in green flame,
The white blossom of spring.

Great trees stand still and shining,
Dew lies on leaf and stone.
In this timeless hour of beauty
The white magic has grown.

The light in the heart of the earth
Flows to the light above;
This is the symbol, the secret,
The pure wellspring of love.

JOAN PUNCHARD

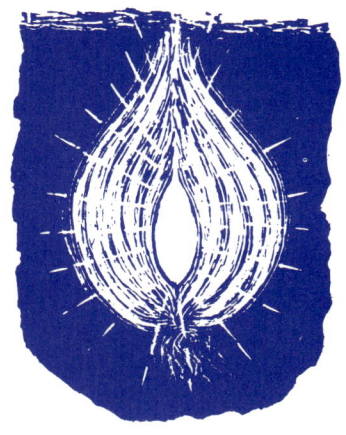

A SHETLAND HOME

This poem was written after the author was asked what her period of living on the Shetland Isles had meant to her. While she records the Shetland landscape, the wind, the long midsummer days with the Sun barely setting, the long midwinter nights lit up sometimes by the Northern Lights ('the skirts of the maiden'), the poem is also about how her years on Shetland were a time when 'her soul found her feet'.
    (The way the poem is set out is influenced by the pattern of Old English verse. A sea-voe is the Shetland word for a sea loch or fjord.)

This land is the Rock   where my soul found her feet.
Leaning into the gale   force Ten
Our bodies the tree-trunks   land lacks no longer;
Learning tenacity   wind grows us roots.
We alone dare   to stand high on the hill.
High noon for us here lasts all summer long, as
The bright face of Morning   shows over the voe-head
Northerly rising and northerly   setting, traversing wholly
The circle of heaven,   compassing sight, heart
And links with humanity.

Midnight is deep, long;   nadir of the long year.
To drink of the dark cup   snuffs all outer sense;
In our ears, ringing   brings us to the circling
Of light in the dark   purple skies.
Majestic the dancing   the skirts of the maiden,
World deva in blues   green and silver
Sweeping the ways   between us and the stars.

Hard rock we scratch to grow corn
for our bodies;
Under the heather lies fuel
for our hearths;
Here on the shore the wrack and the godsend
harbour the treasures
to bring peace of mind.

So now listen, beyond   the soughing of wind,
its keen advancement;   beyond thrud of breakers
on broken sea-shore;   hear sea-maa's calling
ancient music, and   catch the eye of
seal-kind seeking   love - our human love,
so long denied.

And where is my Shetland?   through all the high splendour:
Of sea-voes still   as a mirror of ice,
Reflecting the grass-blades,   path of the sun;
Of high air, great skies   bowing sea-wards
And touching the brows   encircling the crowns
Of we children   who stand on the hill;
Through all of this splendour, I turn at the days end,
Walk with my hoe from the long tattie field,
Pass sheep, sleepy, grazing, as starlings stand
Perched on their backs; my foot stirs a rabbit,
Brown, soft and so fearing,   the dog by my side is a swift
                                        streak of light
And the house on the hill, small and white   the lum reeking,
In circle of light,
Is my home; I shall sleep safely tonight.

ELYAN (PAT STEPHENS)

TAMMY

Tammy, it is your life I would sing,
Not your death and burial. . . .
A life that was related in incidents to me
Tale by thoughtful tale
Pieced together by the tea-cup
And over the tractor wheel;
By the side of crooies at the clipping

And in the high still air of
Flaa Hill, between tuskar strokes.

It was after we'd set the tatties,
Sat warm in-bye, taking soup,
That you spoke of your son.
How he fell between ship and shore.
A promising sea-man.
Your only child.
Soon after, your wife crept into her bell-jar.

You had lived alone now,
Eating your kippers off the Shetland Times
(makes a fine blaze with the oil)
And keeping the cow-byre spotless.

A methodical man with a daily routine
And the seasonal round,
Keeping the fire in, storing
The peats. . . .
Broken by the hope of a helpmeet
A young neighbour wife
Who never would marry
You or anyman else.

You died last November
Strong legs, straight back
Carry you elsewhere
With new lessons to learn.
Here we still learn the steadfastness,
Depth of commitment to truth
In life and season
You taught by your simplicity.

ELYAN (PAT STEPHENS)

REMEMBRANCE

I shall remember only happy things -
Joys shared and loved; the dear delight
Of seagulls drifting on their curved white wings
Against a clear blue sky; the sight
Of moonbeams gleaming on a quiet pool;
Sunset and sunrise; flowers and tall trees
Swaying gently where the wind blows cool;
Long shadows; cloud shapes on calm seas.

I shall remember all the shining things -
Your smile, your eyes, the twinkling light,
Shining with laughter; my heart sings
With joys remembered of the flight
Of dragonflies - the dew - the rain.
Within this shining, you will come again.

JOANNE ATTERBURY

MANY MANSIONS

My heart is God's house.
In God's house are many mansions:
You dwell therein - and you - and you.
Close neighbours are sometimes
Disturbing to each other,
But I love you all;
And here in my heart - God's house -
In peace and harmony you live.

JOANNE ATTERBURY

On the next four pages are poems about the experience of meditation

THE HOUSE OF THE STAR

To the house of the star
The children return once more,
Each following swiftly after
Through the ancient door.
The rooms are filled with their laughter,
Joy that was known before.

The fields lie still in dawn.
A secret wonder is there,
Light falls on the dew-cold grass,
The rose burns clear,
And the mist-shadows rise and pass,
Magic of earth and air.

To come to our true home
We travel far.
In this time of solitude
We know each what we are.
Each is restored, renewed,
In the pure light of the star.

JOAN PUNCHARD

THE CENTRE

In the still bright garden
In the land a child once knew
The light wells and rises,
A flame, a shining dew.

Under the dreaming branch
Crystal clear the grass.
Stillness of full summer,
Beauty that will not pass.

Here shadow has become light,
Held by those heavenly powers.
Here the white fountain shines
And the golden tree flowers.

                    JOAN PUNCHARD

THE LIGHT

Still, calm blue water
A pool of quietness.
No motion, ripples cause. . . .
Here is Thy peace.
'Peace I give unto you
Let go all stress -
I AM . . . find My Peace. . . .
In stillness'

Lord, we kneel in wonder
Before this timeless Light;
We feel Thy grace
Here, the reflection of Thy Face,
All love. . . .
All is One - with realms above
I am a part,
In stillness I find
YOU are within my heart!

JOAN TEE

THE RETURN

Closed in the sleeping earth,
Where stone and dreams endure,
Shines in that hidden place
A flame intense and pure.

Boughs of blossom and light,
Crystal and rose and fire,
In the heart of the wood
Burns on the soul's desire.

The star sealed deep within
Shines to the star above,
Form of stillness and joy,
Image of heavenly love.

JOAN PUNCHARD

MONTSÉGUR

'The Cathars (Albigenses in France) were a mystical religious movement which is believed to have been founded by John (of the fourth Gospel). Their doctrine spread throughout southern Europe from the east early in the eleventh century, and Montségur, a castle on a pinnacle of rock in the foothills of the Pyrenees, was one of their strongholds. In the thirteenth century the Catholic Church mounted a crusade against them and at Montségur they suffered their most devastating defeat after a long siege. Many were walled up alive in the mountain caves, others were burned in the valley below.
    The cornerstone of their faith was the Consolamentum, a magical rite which conferred inspiration and illumination on the recipient. This was often requested on the deathbed and, being a profound expression of the Holy Spirit, raised the consciousness of the dying into the real world. Those who received the Consolamentum in full health became adepts, and led ascetic lives in service to all people, seeming to have an aura about them of supreme love.
    I first visited Montségur in 1978, in ignorance of its history, yet experienced, from within the most frightening circumstances, the peace which lives on in the very rocks and air; the power to overcome all fear.
    The story of the beginnings of the White Eagle Lodge contains associations with Montségur, and many members feel a strong inner link with the Albigenses and have far memories of that time.'

Climbing the pinnacle of rock the light spreads,
As flames once leapt in pyres, so we spiral
Round the dark earth face,
Leaving the valley floor, where cowbells and cicadas
Weave the air into a spell of sound.
We move beyond these temporal things
Into the world of mountains.

For a while the drum of the heartbeat pervades,
Adrenalin rising like panic, and the way steep with stones;
The boulders of life; our pain singing,
And then the castle grows out of the rocks around us,
And I do not wish to stop,
Drawn on a timeless, rushing wave
I climb the ramparts to the south
And sit, legs dangling, before the silent peaks.

And Oh what stillness forms around me!
Fear falls beneath my feet, and the eternal peace,
Beyond all understanding, grows in my heart.

I am there still;

Though distance separates the senses
And other journeys intervene,
The smoke has cleared and tears
Of love now heal the pastures.
Nothing has ended:
The Spirit lives in every pebble on the hillside;
In every moment of the stillness,
Or breath of wind across my cheek,
Conferred by the touch of death -
Consolamentum est.

         PAT DACRE

BROTHER FAITHFUL

Brother Faithful (Ivan Cooke) passed into the world of light in 1981. We are now so often aware of him, strong and youthful, often bringing a feeling a little like that contained in the words of White Eagle's prayer, 'Great White Spirit of eternity, infinity, we are enfolded in Thy great heart, we rest our heart upon Thy heart'. This poem was written in the final year of his earthly life, when his physical body and mind were failing, but somehow almost because of this an inner gentleness seemed to shine forth. The two scraperboard drawings are by Brother Faithful himself.

> I looked at your hands.
> Long, slender, delicately transparent
> tenuous in their physical hold
> Yet full of spiritual strength.
> They shone with healing gold.

Contact tender with strong heat,
your fingers held my palm
and slowly I felt seeping through me
Your golden calm.

> Eyes of blue tranquillity
> denied alertness
> Yet your hands
> showed your world healing thoughts.
> Gold shines all around,

and you stirred something
deep within my heart.

And I felt a nearness
of tenderness and love.
It was not strange
but a timeless feeling of compassionate
certainty that the world was held fast
in Golden Light,
and that you knew it.

    In touching you, for that brief still second
    I knew it too and I loved you because
    You were infinitely lovable and suddenly,
    but absolutely very dear to me.
    The Golden Light shines in your peace and contentment
    And the untidy tackle of old age doesn't matter -
    All that matters is your stillness and harmony.

I looked into your hands,
gently working, and I thought only of healing.
I saw in your hands pulsating
A golden rose of wisdom's perfect harmony.

                                      MARGARET BENTLEY

TO A ROBIN

A little flame you were on dark brown soil,
so quiet and trustingly you looked at me;
I stood quite still - resting my spade a while
and tenderness flowed from my heart to yours.
So was a friendship formed.

You often sat in the old ash nearby
singing to me your dear sweet song of joy,
a song like liquid silver, making my soul
reverberate with longing, aching love
for Him who loves you too.

And once you had to learn the painful lesson
that glass is not like air and you were caught.
I was astonished that my soothing words
made you sit still to let me scoop you up.
You chirped your thanks and flew.

One day your little form lay still
and tooth and claw had ended your sweet song.
As sorrow and rebellion rose in me
I heard the inner voice, reminding me
that God is all Love.

My inner eye then saw you, little friend,
borne up and up into the blazing sun
and with a peaceful folding of the wing
you sat and sang to our Lord your song
of gratitude and love.

CHRISTA FORBES

RESURGENCE

Wield happiness like a sword!
Smash up darkness with a flash of joy!

Fear crumbles.
Laughter rises on the ashes of hate,
shaking the world with new birth pangs.

Uncoil, heart -
Open, mind -
your freedom shall give the years their splendour.

Shout Resurgam!
Trumpet the sun!

                    JOYCE R. NAYLOR

AT CLOSE OF DAY

At close of day
The healers spin their web of healing light
Around the earth.
You who are tired and sick
And wearied of your life
Could, did you know,
Tune into that bright beam
And in the soothing rays of healing light
Find peace and sweet repose
At close of day.

                    ASHTON CLARKE

A PRAYER AT CHRISTMAS

Let the Child of Christ grow in my heart,
The seed grow in my soul,
Let Love become my ruling light,
And wisdom, born of old.
For I have striven with the dark,
And suffered from the cold,
And weary now, I crave the sight
Of heaven's true gold.

Yet as my heart receives the Babe
Another need unfolds;
To nourish *all* the lonely world,
Till each their Star behold.

PAT DACRE